Food and Cooking in...
Ancient Greece

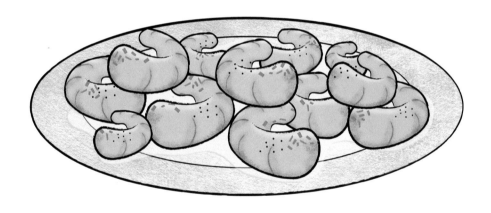

Written by **Clive Gifford**

Illustrations by **Paul Cherrill**

WAYLAND

First published in 2009 by Wayland

Copyright © Wayland 2009

Wayland
Hachette Children's Books
338 Euston Road
London NW1 3BH

Wayland Australia
Level 17/207 Kent Street
Sydney NSW 2000

Series Editor: Victoria Brooker
Editor: Susie Brooks
Designer: Jason Billin
Picture researcher: Shelley Noronha
Food consultant: Stella Sargeson

Picture acknowledgements: Cover and 24, 12, 20, 27 akg-images/Erich Lessing; 4 The Art Archive/Neil Setchfield; 6 The Art Archive/Museo di Villa Giulia Rome/Gianni Dagli Orti; 7 © David Lees/CORBIS; 8 Hervé Champollion/akg-images; 9 British Museum, London, UK/The Bridgeman Art Library; 10 The Art Archive/Archaeological Museum Istanbul/Gianni Dagli Orti; 14 The Art Archive/Cyprus Museum Nicosia/Gianni Dagli Orti; 16, 18 The Art Archive/National Archaeological Museum Athens /Gianni Dagli Orti; 21 The Art Archive/Gianni Dagli Orti; 22 The Art Archive/Bibliothèque des Arts Décoratifs Paris/Gianni Dagli Orti; 23 akg-images; 26 akg-images/Nimatallah; 28 The Art Archive/Museo Nazionale Taranto/Gianni Dagli Orti; 29 akg-images/Bildarchiv Steffens

British Library Cataloguing in Publication Data
Gifford, Clive
Food and cooking in ancient Greece
1. Cookery, Greek - Juvenile literature
2. Food habits - Greece - History - Juvenile literature
I. Title 641.5'938

ISBN: 978 0 7502 5665 0

Printed and bound in China

Wayland is a division of Hachette Children's Books, an Hachette UK Company.

www.hachette.co.uk

Contents

The glorious Greeks

Greece is famous for its hills, islands and beaches – and also its amazing history. Thousands of years ago, one of the first and most important civilisations of Europe grew up there. It began in a period called the Dark Ages (around 1110–800 BCE), and the people responsible were the ancient Greeks.

Towns and cities

The ancient Greeks built many towns and cities. At first, people lived and farmed in the countryside and used the towns only for trade – or for protection if their region came under attack. But by the 400s BCE, larger settlements, like Corinth, had almost 100,000 inhabitants, and Athens (the largest of all) had over 250,000. These cities ruled their surrounding countryside as **city-states**, called *polis*.

▼ *The remains of the theatre of Herodes Atticus built in the centre of Athens. The ancient Greeks were masterful architects and builders.*

Colonies abroad

From around 700 BCE, many Greeks began to move overseas to set up **colonies** along the coasts of the Mediterranean and the Black Sea. These included Syracuse in Sicily, Malaca (now Malaga) in Spain and Odessos (now Odessa) in the Ukraine. The colonies helped to boost trade for the ancient Greeks by supplying foreign foodstuffs and providing new customers for Greek goods.

End of an era

War was common in ancient Greece, as people fought for power. By 336 BCE, the city-states had been conquered by the Greek king Alexander the Great, and 180 years later by the ancient Romans. The ancient Greek civilisation was at its peak for only a few hundred years, but it had enormous influence on the Romans and others in Europe and the Middle East. The Greeks made great advances in science, politics, philosophy, the arts and education. Many of their legacies, from the Olympic Games to foods and recipes, are with us to this day.

▲ This map shows ancient Greece (circa 650-30 BCE) and its colonies.

Earlier civilisations

People have lived in Greece since **prehistoric** times. The ancient Greeks followed on from two earlier civilisations – the Minoans on the island of Crete and the Mycenaeans on the Greek mainland.

Food from the farm

Ancient Greece had a sunny **climate**, but the rugged, dry landscape with many hills, mountains and forests made farming tough. Only certain crops flourished – the most important being olives, grapes and barley.

Cereal seasons

Barley grew better in Greece than wheat, and so it was the main cereal crop. Planting took place in late September or October, by which time the land had baked hard in the summer sun. Farmers used a simple wooden plough and a hoe to break up the soil, before sowing the seed by hand.

In late spring or early summer, the crop would be harvested using a **sickle**. Work animals such as donkeys and mules were used to trample the barley to separate the grain from the stalks. Then the grain was ground into flour.

Olives, grapes and honey

Many farmers planted olive groves and vineyards of grapes, mainly for producing olive oil and wine. Wine makers would crush the grapes by foot and then leave them to **ferment** for many months. The ancient Greeks also kept bees for making honey – a popular sweetener, as sugar was unknown at the time.

▶ *This clay **amphora** shows a man drinking wine in a vineyard.*

Growing greens

Ancient Greek herbs included oregano, sage, thyme, marjoram and mustard. These might be grown in a vegetable garden along with beans, chickpeas, lentils, cabbages and onions. Some households had orchards of trees bearing figs and nuts. Other food plants, such as celery and fennel, were gathered from the wild.

Keeping animals

There was little grassland for grazing cattle. Instead, most ancient Greek farmers kept small herds of goats or sheep – mainly for their milk. Families living near woods or forests often kept pigs for meat, whilst chickens and geese provided eggs.

▲ Artemis was the Greek goddess of hunting and wild animals. Here she is shown giving food to a goat.

Soil secrets

To keep the soil **fertile**, some Greeks practised a simple form of crop rotation, leaving an area of land unplanted one year and then growing a crop there the next. They built **irrigation** systems with wells, water tanks and channels to carry water to their sun-dried fields.

The importance of olives

Olives proved to be incredibly important fruits in ancient Greece. They were used not just in cookery, but also in cleaning and cosmetics.

Olive trees everywhere

Olive trees may have first appeared in Turkey, Lebanon and the eastern Mediterranean, but the ancient Greeks were the first to **cultivate** olives and produce olive oil. Greece's hot, dry climate was perfect for growing this sun-loving fruit.

Collecting the crop

The olive harvest took place from late autumn to the beginning of winter. Farmers either picked the fruits by hand or used a long wooden pole to knock them out of the trees onto a cloth spread on the ground. Some olives were eaten, stored or traded whole, but most of the crop was pressed to create olive oil. This was stored in large clay jars called amphorae.

▶ *Olive trees still grow next to the fortress wall that separated the Greek city-states of Attica and Boeotia.*

Feeding the nation

The Greek **philosopher**, Sophocles, called the olive tree 'the tree that feeds the children'. Olives and olive oil formed a vital part of many ancient Greeks' diets and were a key source of fat. Olive oil featured in many cooked dishes, and was also used alone as a dip for bread.

More than food

Olive oil had many uses other than for food. The ancient Greeks had no soap, so people rubbed on olive oil and then scraped it off to keep clean. Some women also used the oil as a moisturiser for their skin. Olive oil was used as a fuel to light clay lanterns, or glass ones if you were wealthy. Ancient Greek writings also list over 60 medical uses for olive oil, including treating small wounds and severe fevers.

▲ *This amphora shows olives being harvested. Foods stored in amphorae were often topped with a layer of olive oil to help keep the air out and preserve the food.*

Olives at the Olympics

Many athletes at the ancient Olympic Games (see page 29) massaged themselves in olive oil to tone their muscles. The winners of Olympic events were crowned with a wreath made out of wild olive branches, called a *kotinos*. Back home, Olympic champions often received many amphorae of olive oil as a valuable prize for their success.

Breakfast and lunch

During the sunny summers in Greece, no one wanted to eat hot, heavy meals. Even in winter, the ancient Greeks had just one hot meal a day in the evening. At other times, they usually ate simple mixtures of cold foods.

Breakfast

The first meal of the day was breakfast, or *akratisma*. Whether they were rich or poor, most Greeks ate bread dipped in strong wine, sometimes with a few olives or figs. Greek flour, usually made from barley, produced rough flatbreads or barley cakes, called *maza*.

Midday meal

Ariston was lunch, taken at midday or in the early afternoon. It was similar to breakfast, but often with extra olives, dried and fresh fruits, vegetables and cheeses or yoghurt made from goats' or sheep's milk. The ancient Greeks drank water or milk with their meals – or occasionally wine, mixed with water to make it weaker. In winter, hot water, wine and honey would be blended to make a warming drink.

◀ *A large family sit down for a meal in this stone carving from the 3rd century BCE.*

Barley cakes and tzatziki

This modern version of the ancient Greek *maza* adds herbs for extra flavour.
Instead of wine, you can dip it in oil and tzatziki.

Serves 2–4

You will need:

200g barley flour
3 tablespoons clear honey
1 teaspoon thyme or marjoram
2 tablespoons olive oil
100ml water
Extra flour for rolling dough

For the dips:

100g feta cheese
40ml olive oil
1 teaspoon white wine vinegar
1 garlic clove
Small pot Greek yoghurt
Black pepper

1. Crush the garlic. Mix with 2 teaspoons of olive oil, the vinegar and pepper. Now mix the yoghurt in with the other ingredients and leave to cool in the fridge for at least an hour. This is the tzatziki.

2. Mix together the flour, honey, herbs and olive oil in a bowl. Add the water, little by little, and mix until a dough is formed.

3. Cool the dough in the fridge for 10 minutes while you heat the oven to 200°C. Then roll out the dough on a lightly floured surface, until it is about 5mm thick.

4. Cut out 10cm-wide circles of dough and place on a greased baking tray. Bake in the oven for about 15–20 minutes.

5. Crumble the feta cheese onto a saucer. Pour the olive oil onto another saucer.

6. Serve the barley cakes warm, dipping them into the tzatziki or into the olive oil and then into the cheese.

11

Evening meal

Deipnon (or *Dorpon*) was the ancient Greeks' evening meal. At home, it was usually a simple serving of soup or stew, sometimes followed by dried figs, cakes and cheese.

Doing the cooking

An ordinary family dinner would be cooked by the women of the house or, in wealthier households, by female slaves. On special occasions, professional cooks might be hired. Some cooks insisted on bringing their own kitchen staff as well.

Serving up

Food was mostly served in bowls, placed at a low wooden table. The ancient Greeks used their fingers instead of knives or forks. They ate soups and stews with a spoon or a piece of bread scooped out in the shape of a spoon.

▲ *Cooking was considered women's work and was long and tiring. This terracotta statue shows a woman stirring a saucepan with a long ladle.*

Men-only

Many ancient Greek men ate separately from women and children, often in a dedicated room called an *andron*. This was the most luxuriously furnished room of a Greek home. The women's area of a house was called the *gynaeceum* or *gunaikeion*.

Baked fish with feta

This recipe comes from one of the earliest known cookbooks, *Art of Cookery*, written by an ancient Greek called Mithaecus. He used bass, but you can use any type of fish fillet.

Serves 4

You will need:

1 tablespoon fresh chives
1 tablespoon fresh dill
50g feta cheese

50g breadcrumbs
1 tablespoon olive oil
4 medium-to-large fillets of fish
Salt and black pepper

1. Preheat the oven to around 190°C. Chop up the herbs as finely as you can.

2. Crumble the feta cheese and mix it with the herbs and breadcrumbs before adding the oil.

3. Sprinkle salt and pepper over each of the fish fillets and place them on a greased baking tray.

4. Top with the breadcrumb mixture and press it into the fish.

5. Bake in the oven until the fish is cooked thoroughly. This should take around 20 minutes, but check after 15 minutes. Serve with fresh salad or steamed vegetables.

Home cooking

Wealthy ancient Greeks had large kitchens, staffed by many slaves. But most families cooked using a simple open fire, with various devices for baking, roasting or grilling.

The open fire

The cooking fire was often built in the courtyard of a house, or out on the street. If neighbours had a large fire going, they might be asked to share a part of it. Some foods, such as fish, would be wrapped and placed in the flames to cook. But the ancient Greeks had other ways of cooking too.

Flame-grilling

The *eschara* was a small, raised grill. It was made of metal and had four short legs to allow it to stand over the fire. Meats, fish and other items could be grilled on it above the flames, much like a modern barbecue.

In the oven

The ancient Greeks also had a type of oven, called a *kribanos*. This was used to bake bread and cakes, as well as for roasting meats and fish. A *kribanos* was made of clay, with a small door or hatch to access the food and often short, stubby legs to rest in the fire. Coals could be placed around the oven to help spread out the heat. Many *kribanos* were portable and could be carried to wherever a fire was blazing.

▼ *Ancient Greek cooking utensils were made of **terracotta** or **bronze**. This bronze cauldron could be heated to high temperatures without breaking.*

Souvlakia

This meat-on-skewers dish is still popular in Greece. In ancient times, it would have been cooked on an *eschara*, but you can use a barbecue, a grill or even a griddle pan.

Serves 4 as a starter, 2 as a main meal

You will need:

4 garlic cloves

1 medium onion

1 teaspoon oregano

2 tablespoons olive oil

150ml white grape juice

Pinch of salt

$\frac{1}{2}$ teaspoon black pepper

400g boneless lamb or chicken

4 skewers

1. Peel the garlic cloves and crush them. Grate the onion and place with the garlic and oregano in a mixing bowl.

2. Add the olive oil, grape juice and salt and pepper and mix thoroughly. This is the marinade.

3. Cut the meat into 2cm cubes and add to the marinade, making sure all the meat is coated. Leave in a fridge overnight, or for at least 3 hours.

4. Thread the meat cubes onto the skewers. Make sure you leave a gap between each cube to allow all sides of the meat to cook.

5. Heat a grill, barbecue or griddle pan and cook the skewers of meat for 10–15 minutes. Turn the meat occasionally and brush with some of the spare marinade.

6. Check the meat is cooked through by removing one cube from a skewer and cutting it in two. When ready, serve with salad and a dollop of Greek yoghurt.

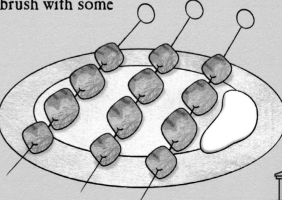

Seafood

Greece has one of the longest coastlines in the world. The waters provided rich fishing grounds and an important source of food for many ancient Greeks.

Fruits of the sea

The ancient Greeks caught and ate many types of fish, from sardines and red mullet to mackerel and eels. They also enjoyed seafood, including prawns, squid, octopus and mussels.

Treasured tuna

Mediterranean tuna were highly prized. Tuna watchers would climb tall cliffs or wooden towers to spot shoals of tuna and signal to fishermen in boats. Most fishermen caught tuna in nets, although one technique was to drop big chunks of wood with spikes sticking out to spear young fish.

▲ *This ancient painting shows a fisherman displaying his large catch of fish.*

Fishy dishes

Fish was often served in grilled slices called *temakhos*. The ancient Greeks also preserved fish by drying it in the hot sun, or salting or pickling it to create *tarikhos*. Preserved fish was traded all around the Mediterranean. Sometimes, fish would be served with sour grapes to give it a sharp taste.

Spiky starters

Some ancient Greeks were fond of eating *echinous* – sea urchins that were found in large numbers along many rocky shorelines. They were caught and caked in mud before being baked. Once cooked, their spiny shell could be peeled off easily.

Honey-glazed prawns

The Mediterranean sea was full of large prawns, which the ancient Greeks loved. This simple dish uses typical ingredients of the time.

Serves 2

You will need:

1½ tablespoons olive oil
1½ tablespoons honey
200g cooked, cleaned shrimps

1 tablespoon fresh oregano,
   finely chopped
Black pepper

1. Mix together the oil and honey and place in a frying pan or skillet.

2. Add the shrimps to the pan and cook for 3–4 minutes until they are soft.

3. Remove the shrimps and boil the remaining liquid for 2 minutes, adding the oregano after 1 minute.

4. Pour the sauce over the shrimps and sprinkle with black pepper. Eat immediately.

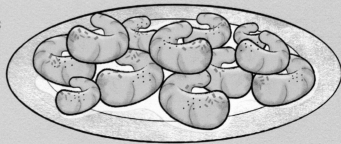

Rich and poor

In ancient Greek towns and cities, there was a great difference between the foods available for the rich and for the poor.

Meagre meals

Meat and fish were usually far too expensive for poorer Greeks to buy regularly. Instead, poor families cooked soups and stews using vegetables and **legumes** like beans and lentils, which are high in **protein**. Other key sources of protein for poorer Greeks were cheese and eggs. Fresh vegetables in cities were expensive, but most people could afford dried or pickled varieties. Grainy porridges and rough barley breads were also common foods.

▲ *A typical ancient Greek townhouse was made of mud bricks with small holes in the wall for windows.*

Wealth of choice

The rich had a far more varied diet, including fresh meats, shellfish, and expensive breads and cakes made from wheat. Slaves were sent to the agora (see pages 20–21) or a city's **docks** to buy exotic spices from Asia and the Middle East, figs and sweet wines from Syria and dates from North Africa. They might also bring home luxuries such as fresh belly of tuna, oysters and **caviar**.

Daring dinners

A dinner for wealthy ancient Greeks might include some interesting favours. Popular delicacies were pig's belly flavoured in herbs and vinegar, peacock's eggs, roasted hare and iris bulbs soaked in vinegar.

Faikes (lentil soup)

Lentils are very high in protein, and lentil soups were popular among the poor of ancient Greece. This recipe makes a thick and filling soup.

Serves 4

You will need:

225g small green or
      brown lentils
5 garlic cloves
1 carrot
450ml water

1 medium onion
50ml olive oil
2 x 400g tins chopped tomatoes
2 bay leaves
Salt and black pepper

1. Place the lentils in a large saucepan, cover with water, bring to the boil and boil for 5 minutes, making sure the water always covers the lentils.

2. Drain the lentils thoroughly, then put them back in the pan with 450ml of fresh water. Bring to the boil and simmer for 10 minutes.

3. Peel and finely chop the garlic. Chop the carrot and onion into small pieces.

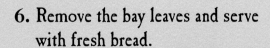

4. Add these, along with the olive oil, tinned tomatoes and bay leaves, to the pan.

5. Stir the soup regularly and sprinkle in the salt and pepper. Cook on a low heat for 45–60 minutes until all the ingredients are tender.

6. Remove the bay leaves and serve with fresh bread.

At the agora

Most ancient Greek towns and cities revolved around a central square called the agora. People came here to meet each other and to shop at bustling markets.

Bordered by buildings

An ancient Greek agora was usually shaped like a rectangle. Around the edge were long buildings with many columns and covered walkways for people to stroll under. These buildings were called *stoa* and often housed lots of shops and craft workshops. Other important buildings, such as law courts, stood nearby.

Centre stage

In the middle of the agora there were often statues of famous leaders, sportsmen or gods. Trees were planted to provide shade, and some people would meet under their branches to discuss politics and other matters, while others wandered the agora looking for work.

► Pastry sellers would wander ancient Greek agoras trying to sell their wares whilst they were still warm and fresh.

Off to market

Most people went to the agora to buy food and other goods from the dozens of market stalls. These sold clothing, sandals, fruit, vegetables, honey, wine and cooking equipment. Fresh meat and fish were displayed on marble slabs, which helped to keep the food cool. Farm livestock, donkeys and slaves were also put on display and sold.

Regular trade

Ancient Greek men or their slaves were the most common shoppers. Women rarely bought food, but might visit the agora to collect water from a public fountain or, if wealthy, shop for perfumes and other luxury goods. Officials called *metronomoi* made sure the weights used in the markets were fair. They checked market traders' weights against their own standard set.

▲ *The ancient Greek shopping arcade, the Stoa of Attalus, has been restored and sits along one side of the giant agora at Athens.*

The Athens agora

Athens was the largest city in ancient Greece, and its agora was extremely impressive. Hundreds of stalls, booths and shops stood in groups, according to the type of goods they sold. The law courts and prison were next door, and any citizen of Athens in the agora could be forced to join the **jury** if a law case was going on.

Trading by sea

As ancient Greece developed, it grew in power and wealth. The varying city-states began trading more and more with each other as well as looking further afield for food, flavourings and other items.

Bring on the boats

Mainland Greece is mountainous and difficult to cross, and many ancient Greeks lived on islands. For these reasons, people travelled mostly by sea. From around 800 BCE, Greek trade flourished right across the Mediterranean. Ships powered by sails and oars were a common sight, ferrying food and other goods to and from ports.

Buying and selling

The ancient Greeks traded their local goods, particularly olives, olive oil, wine, and crafts such as pottery and jewellery. Sometimes precious metals and captured slaves were also sold. In return, Greek traders sought many foreign items, from cheese, pork and grain from Sicily, to Persian peaches, timber from Macedonia and smoked fish from Spain. Pepper and spices, cinnamon and other flavourings often came from the Middle East.

▶ *Many Greek cargo ships used both sails and large numbers of rowers pulling oars.*

Cereal shopping

A number of the Greek city-states were very rocky, making it difficult to grow large fields of crops. These places relied on trade from the sea to supply enough grain for their numerous breads, cakes and porridges.

Ship storage

Trading ships were often manned by slaves and carried goods stored in wooden barrels and amphorae. These containers kept out the damp, as well as pests such as mice and rats. They were often wrapped in straw to stop them breaking and lashed together in groups. Many traders sold their **cargoes** in the port, with merchants buying portions to trade at the local market.

▼ *Greek ports and docks were a hive of activity with slaves loading and unloading ships and traders negotiating the buying and selling of cargoes.*

The port of Piraeus

One of the biggest ports in ancient Greece was Piraeus, which served the city-state of Athens. It is estimated that 70,000–100,000 tonnes of grain may have arrived on 400–600 ships to feed Athens every year!

At the *symposium*

Ancient Greek society was dominated by men. Women weren't allowed to vote – or attend drinking parties, which often followed dinner. These drinking parties were called *symposia*.

Evening entertainment

Ancient Greek men would gather at a *symposium* to drink wine and discuss important matters, or just to party and play games. There were often speeches and poems, and sometimes dancers, acrobats or musicians, to entertain the guests. Popular men, such as famous thinkers or people of wealth or power, might move from one *symposium* to another throughout the evening.

King of the banquet

To host the occasion, a 'king of the banquet' called a *symposiarch* was chosen. He would decide which wines to offer and how much water should be added to dilute them. Wine was poured from a large jar called a *krater* into shallow drinking bowls or cups, called *kylixes*.

▲ Guests at a symposium would sit or lie on couches or wall seats, eating, drinking and talking while slaves handed round snacks or poured wine.

Kottabos

One of the most popular games at a *symposium* was *kottabos*. This involved a man flicking his wrist to send a small amount of wine flying from his cup towards a target. Sometimes there was a prize for the winner.

Honey sesame fritters

These delicious fritters were typical snacks at an ancient Greek *symposium*.

Serves 2 as a snack

You will need:

20g sesame seeds
125g flour
225ml water

2–3 tablespoons honey
olive oil
kitchen towel

1. Pre-heat the oven to 180°C. Place the sesame seeds on a baking tray and bake for a couple of minutes. Place in a saucer.

2. Sift the flour into a bowl and make a well in the centre. Slowly add the water and 1 tablespoon of honey, stirring as you go until you have a runny dough.

3. Heat 2 tablespoons of olive oil in a small frying pan and pour in around a quarter of the dough mixture. As it cooks, it will thicken.

4. Turn the fritter over several times to brown both sides. Remove from the pan and place it on a kitchen towel on a plate. Repeat with the other portions of the mixture.

5. Pour the remaining honey over the fritters. Use tongs to pick up each fritter and coat it in the sesame seeds. Eat while still warm, with your fingers or a fork.

Beliefs and worship

The ancient Greeks were keen philosophers and thinkers, with a variety of beliefs. Most people worshipped a great number of gods, who influenced different aspects of their lives.

Great gods

The 12 most important Greek gods were the Olympians, who ruled from Mount Olympus. Most powerful of all was Zeus. He had two brothers – Poseidon, god of the sea, and Hades, god of the **underworld**. Zeus's wife and sister, Hera was the goddess of women and of marriage, while Demeter controlled the seasons, farming and nature. The ancient Greeks told many stories about their gods, known as **myths**.

The acropolis

Temples to the gods were usually built on a high hill in a town, called an **acropolis**. These temples were often dedicated to just one god – for example, the Parthenon in Athens was built for the goddess of wisdom and crafts, Athena, from where the city gets its name.

▶ *This temple at the acropolis in Athens is dedicated to Nike, the ancient Greek goddess of victory. People would visit the temple, in the hope of defeating enemies in battle.*

Temple worship

Ancient Greek temples were rarely places where people went inside to worship. Instead, they tended to house a statue or image of an important god. People would make offerings outside, including gold, stone sculptures or foods such as wine, honey, wheat and the first fruit from a tree.

Animal offerings

Animals such as cattle, sheep and chickens were often **sacrificed** to please the gods, in the hope that this would improve people's lives or help them stay peaceful and happy. Fishermen would often sacrifice a large tuna to honour Poseidon, their most important god. The fishermen of Boetia in central Greece sacrificed eels, placing wreaths over them and sprinkling them with barley.

▼ *Important farm animals were sometimes sacrificed to honour a god. This vase shows a valuable bull shortly before it is about to be sacrificed.*

Strict diets

Some ancient Greeks believed it was wrong to kill and eat animals and became vegetarians to keep their bodies and minds pure. They included a religious group known as the Orphics and the famous philosophers Plato and Pythagoras.

Festivals and contests

The ancient Greeks believed that their gods enjoyed food, feasts and ceremonies as much as they did. **Festivals** to honour the gods became an important part of life.

Special celebrations

Many festivals included prayers, singing and ritual dances, as well as eating and drinking. Animals were sacrificed, with the least edible parts offered to the god and the tastiest parts cooked and eaten by the festival-goers.

Calendar events

Festivals happened year-round. In February or March, people in Athens celebrated *Anthesteria*, a three-day festival to Dionysus, god of wine. On the first day, wine casks were opened in a room decorated with spring flowers. The wine was drunk on the second day, and on the third day food offerings were made. In October or November, a women-only festival called *Thesmophoria* was held in honour of Demeter, goddess of farming.

▲ *On this vase, people dance during a festival held at Taranto, a Greek colony on the southern coast of Italy which was founded in the 8th century BCE.*

Sporting festivals

Religious festivals involving sports events became very popular, including the Isthmian Games in Corinth and the Pythian Games in Delphi. The most famous of all were the games held at Olympia to honour Zeus. The Olympics, as they became known, began in 776 BCE with just one event – a running race of 180–190 metres, called a **stade**. The first winner was a cook called Coribos.

The Olympic Games

The ancient Olympics were held every four years, for over 1,000 years. They blossomed into a multi-sport event, with tens of thousands of spectators watching running, throwing, jumping and wrestling contests. Olympic champions received just an olive wreath at Olympia, but back home they were often rewarded handsomely with gold or food. In the Greek town of Eleusis, for example, winners were given free sacks of barley.

▲ This vase shows three young men running at an ancient Greek games whilst two judges look on.

Meaty Milon

Many Olympic athletes ate a lot of meat. The legendary Milon of Croton, who won the wrestling competition at five ancient Olympics in a row (532–516 BCE), was said to eat 20 pounds of meat per day! Charmis of Sparta, in contrast, ate almost nothing but dried figs on the way to winning the running race in 688 BCE.

Glossary

acropolis a fortress or guarded area at the top of high ground in a town.

amphora(e) a clay jar, usually with two handles, used by the ancient Greeks to hold wine or oil.

bronze a metal made from mixing copper and tin which was used for weapons and cooking utensils.

cargo the goods, food or raw materials carried on a ship or boat.

caviar fish eggs, eaten as a luxury.

city-state a community with its own government which was usually made up of a large town or city and the surrounding area of farmland.

climate the weather conditions found in a place over a long period of time.

colony a town or area of land ruled by another country.

cultivate to grow plants or prepare soil for planting crops.

docks an area where ships loaded and unloaded their cargoes.

ferment chemical reactions that convert sugar in foods into alcohol.

fertile when used about land, it means that the soil and conditions are good for growing crops.

irrigation a system of channels that supply an area of land with water, particularly to help crops to grow well.

jury a panel of people who decide on the verdict of a case at a court

legume a group of plants which produce fruits in a pod including peas, beans, lentils and clover.

myths stories and tales about imaginary characters and events.

philosopher a person who studies and investigates questions about knowledge and existence.

prehistoric the period in history before there were written records.

protein group of substances essential for human growth and health. Meats, fish, cheese, eggs and nuts are all important sources of protein.

sacrifice to kill a creature or offer food or other goods to honour a god.

sickle a farm tool with a curved blade used for cutting grass or cereal crops.

stade an ancient unit of measurement believed to be 180-190m, which became the name of the first race at the ancient Olympics.

terracotta a type of hard clay used to make pottery and other objects.

underworld according to ancient Greek myths, a place beneath the Earth's surface where the spirits of dead people travelled.

Further information

Books

Facts About the Greeks by Liz Gogerly (Wayland, 2007)
Find Out About Ancient Greece by Colin Hynson (Wayland, 2006)
Gruesome Truth About the Greeks by Jillian Powell (Wayland, 2008)
History Beneath Your Feet: Ancient Greece by Jane Shuter (Wayland, 2008)
Look Around a Greek Temple by Richard Dargie (Watts, 2007)
Men, Women and Children in Ancient Greece by Colin Hynson (Wayland, 2007)
Rich and Poor in Ancient Greece by Stewart Ross (Watts, 2009)

Websites

http://greece.mrdonn.org/index.html
This website contains many different pages on ancient Greek topics including food, homes, religion and gods.

http://www.ancientgreece.co.uk
Learn more about the ancient Greeks and their daily lives at this fascinating website produced by the British Museum.

http://www.museum.upenn.edu/Greek_World/Index.html
An informative website with lots of features on different aspects of ancient Greece, including coins, trade and daily life.

http://www.bbc.co.uk/schools/ancientgreece/olympia/
An interactive introduction to the ancient Olympic Games through the BBC website.

Cooking Conversions

g = gram; ml = millilitre; oz = ounce

			Celsius (°C)	Fahrenheit (°F)	Gas Mark
			130	250	$\frac{1}{2}$
1 teaspoon	$\frac{1}{6}$ oz	5ml	140	275	1
1 tablespoon	$\frac{1}{2}$ oz	15ml	150	300	2
1 fluid ounce	1 oz	30ml	170	325	3
1 US pint	16 oz	475ml	180	350	4
			190	375	5
	50g	$1\frac{1}{2}$ oz	200	400	6
	100g	$3\frac{1}{2}$ oz	220	425	7
	200g	7 oz	230	450	8
	500g	$17\frac{1}{2}$ oz	240	475	9

Index

Food and Cooking in...

Contents of all books in the series:

WAYLAND